In Every Situation,

God Is There

By

Priscilla Bohannon

All illustrations by: Gerry Brasfield "Bras"

New King James Version (NKJV)
"Scripture taken from the New King James Version. Copyright © 1982 by Thomas Nelson, Inc. Used by permission. All rights reserved."

ISBN #ISBN-13: 978-1500642105

ISBN-10: 150064210X

Heart of My Heart Publishing Co., LLC

www.three-sheep.com

In loving memory
of my Father-in-Law,

Dean Bohannon 11/12/43 - 4/14/12

Table of Contents

Preface

When I first felt led to write this book, I didn't think much about baring my feelings to the world. I didn't even know if there was a chance of publishing in the future. As I thought of the possibility, I wondered, "Do I really want to share my heart?" I love to talk to people about the Lord and I know the Lord leads me to- but in book form? Do I want the whole world to know my feelings of despair? Of anguish? Well, why not? Jesus did. He felt alone. He felt agony. He had emotions.

God came down as man. He can relate to us. He was justified in his actions and feelings because He *was* God and He *was* without sin. That's the difference. He didn't sin. We do. The bible says in Romans 3:23 NKJV, "for all have sinned and fall short of the glory of God." Therefore, how much more am I? He's the Savior, I'm a sinner, saved by grace, through faith. (Ephesians 2:8) He shared His feelings, I'll share mine.

Sharing our feelings, mistakes, failures, weaknesses, and struggles often help others. We aren't perfect. We only *want* to be because of what Christ did for us. None of the men or women in the bible were without sin, yet they were used by Him! Look at David, for example. He was real and he made mistakes, but he loved God. 1 Samuel 13:14 NKJV says, "The LORD has sought for Himself a man after His own heart". He was talking about David. Our Father is all knowing and I know He sees into my heart and He sees the intent thereof. I know He loves me, in spite of me and I'm forever grateful. When God looks down at me, I want him to say, "There's a *woman* after My own heart."

Acknowledgments

I want to thank the Lord for all He has done, is doing and is going to do. I'm so grateful that He loves me in spite of me. He always amazes me!

I would like to thank my husband, Jason, my stepson, Eric, and my daughter, Leah, for loving me and accepting me. I have such a deep love for you all.

I'd like to thank my Dad for taking the time to draw the pictures for this book.

My Mom for your love, support, and feedback.

Dad and Mom for loving one another, loving us, teaching us morals and disciplining us. I love you both very much. Proverbs 22:6

I want to thank all of my family-

My brothers- Randy, Ricky and Keith.

My sister- Rebecca. Beck, thanks for praying for a little sister. I'm glad to have been born into this family.

Anytime I've ever needed anything- you all have always gone above and beyond the call to help me in any way you could. I will never forget how much each of you have done for me. I love you all very much and I'm thankful for the time we're able to spend together.

Thank you to my brothers-in-law and sisters-in-law and your families, my aunts, uncles, cousins, nieces, nephews- each and every one. So many of you have done so much for me and I am forever grateful. You're all so special in your own way and I love each and every one of you.

My mother-in-law, Pam, for loving me as your daughter. Ruth 1:16,17

My step father-in-law, Wayne, for your kindness.

Grandpaw, for loving me and helping me throughout the years.

Thank you to my Christian brothers and sisters that have been there for me and shown me much love and encouragement- past and present.

Mr. Fred and Mrs. Barbara Jones for loving me as a daughter. Thank you for all you've taught me and shown me. I'm forever grateful our paths crossed. I love you both very much. Philippians 1:21 & Isaiah 40:31

Thank you, Jody Davis, for helping me so much with this. I can always count on you to give me your honest opinion. You've been such an encouragement. I'm forever grateful for you and I love you!

Ms. Ann (Matthews), thank you for looking over the book, your input and encouragement. I appreciate you and I love you.

Several of you have given me much feedback on the stories in this book. I appreciate the time you have taken to do so. The excitement so many of you have shown has been so encouraging.

All my friends that have prayed for me, encouraged me, accepted me, and supported me throughout my life- I appreciate your friendship, support, and love for me and the Lord's work.

All those that have helped me in any way throughout the years.

So many have touched my life and I'm forever grateful. If I were to sit and name all of you, it would take another book. I love you all.

A special thank you to Theresa Nichols for your prayers, support, love, patience, time, encouragement, and making it possible for this book to be published. May God continue to bless you!

May God continue to bless you all!

A Note from Author

Our heavenly Father's arms are stretched out for us,

Just as His Son, Jesus, had His arms stretched out

for us on the cross.

He's waiting for us to come to Him-

In the good times and the bad.

When we join Him, accepting His will for our lives,

His arms are no longer stretched out.

They are wrapped around us in full embrace,

As well as holding us up.

As He's given me the stories in this book,

God has shown me and He wants to show you-

We're not alone.

In Every Situation,

God is There.

Chapter One

Cleaning the Interior

It was the middle of February and the first beautiful day I'd seen in a while. I didn't have to work so I decided to clean the interior of my car. It had been way too cold to even think about cleaning it lately and it was a mess. It was downright filthy! I vacuumed, wiped down the dash, doors- every inch. I struggled to fit my hand through the crevices that were too small for the vacuum cleaner hose. I was spraying the seats and carpets with cleaner and scrubbing like nobody's business. Trying as hard as I could, I couldn't seem to get the coffee stains out of the carpet right underneath my cup holder where I carelessly spill the coffee from my cup as I scurry through my morning routine.

I looked at the stains that remained. I looked at my hands. They had dirt and small cuts all over them. I had worked vigorously to get it spotless. I was so exhausted. The car looked so much better but it wasn't as I wanted it. Although I had done my best, I had still failed.

As I sat in the passenger seat, I thought of how God sees us before we accept Jesus into our hearts. No matter how hard we try to clean up our "interior," the stains of sin are still there. The only way to rid ourselves of the unsightly appearance of sin is through our acceptance of Jesus. When we genuinely seek Him and ask Him to come into our hearts, we are forgiven. No longer does God see the stains, but He sees the blood of His Son. 1 Peter 1:19 NKJV says "but with the precious blood of Christ, as of a lamb without blemish and without spot."

I'm thankful for those "forever there" coffee stains. They will remind me that I may see them on the interior of the car, but God no longer sees the stains of sin within or upon me.

We often think we can hide or take away our own sin. Saved or unsaved, have you ever tried to clean your "interior" yourself? If you have, being honest with yourself, can or could you tell there's still a heaviness there?

Dear heavenly Father, We come to You in Jesus' name and ask You to forgive us for our sins. We know we sin every day, whether it be by doing something we shouldn't or by not doing something we should. Please help us to remember Your mercy and grace is extended upon us daily. When we see any stain, help us to remember that You no longer see the stain of sin upon us. We are made clean by the blood of Your Son, Jesus, when we accept Him into our hearts. Thank You, Father. In Jesus' name, amen.

Chapter Two

Car Salesman

Although he's now retired, my Dad was a car salesman for about 27 years. His former customers have always told me he was honest. Many of them that I know have bought multiple cars from him because they knew he would treat them right. They respect him for that and so do I. I've recently admitted when going to a car dealership, I have a hard time talking to the salesman. I even have a hard time smiling at them, shaking their hand, and even treating them kind at all! When I admitted it, I realized I wasn't behaving as a Christian and I didn't even need to go to a car lot!

When I was 19, my husband and I decided to look for a car. We looked at what they had at my Dad's place of work. We didn't find anything we were interested in, so we decided to look at some other places. We went out of town one day and pulled into a large car dealership. A young man quickly approached us, not giving much time for us to even pull several feet into the lot. He proceeded to use high-pressure tactics, which caused me great irritability. At first I thought, ok, it's salesmen that are pushy and inexperienced that I don't want to deal with. After more searching, it didn't take me long before I realized I despised *all* car salesmen except my Dad! It didn't matter- young or old, man or woman, energetic or not. Was it because I felt we should always go to my Dad to buy a vehicle? Was it because I knew him and trusted him to treat me honestly? Why would I even *want* to talk to anyone else?

Recently Jason asked me to pull into a dealership parking lot to look at their trucks. As sad is it is to say, I remained in the car because I knew I didn't want to be faced with the salesman. I figured if I can't be nice, don't get out. A man maybe in his late 50's or early 60's came walking across the parking lot. I watched him as he was in what I call the "sneak attack" mode. As he walked across the parking lot toward Jason, I saw the look on his face. I noticed the hesitation. It was almost as if I heard him say, "Why do I have to do this job. I really don't want to approach this guy. I know what he's thinking- here's another used car salesman that's going to try his best to rip me off." I watched him as he prepared for his opening line - "Hello sir, have you found something you're interested in?"

He was uncomfortable, yet he had a job to do. He has to provide a living for himself. I began to picture in my mind, his family. Maybe he's helping one of his children financially. Maybe even his grandchild. His wife may be sick. For all I know, *he* may be sick. It may be the only job he is able to do and he's doing it. This man probably meets so many different kinds of people. Some friendly, some not. Unkind people make your job unbearable at times- and I've been one of those people for a long time! I was so upset to think how rude I'd been in the past. I've been the cause for someone to have a bad day! I realized how disappointed I was at myself for my past behavior. I wasn't a Christian through all these years but I have been for a while. I was hurt that I hurt someone. I was truly ashamed. My heart sank!

At that moment, I realized what I'd been doing. I thought of all the times the Lord had prepared a heart and sent me to talk to someone about Him. I always have that feeling that I'm going to be facing someone like...well, me! I had judged all car salesmen because of their title. I wasn't going to give them a chance because I had a couple of bad experiences with pushy salesmen and I put it into my mind that they were all the same. I treated them terribly and I didn't even know them! I didn't know what they were going through in their lives. What a struggle it may be to provide a living for their family. How nervous they may be at approaching a stranger. How many people had been rude to them that day, just because they had a job to do. Maybe they knew what it was like. Maybe they wanted to change the perception of the job they were called to do, but I didn't give them a chance.

I realized that car salesmen and Christians are a lot alike. There are some that go about selling a car the wrong way as some Christians go about leading someone to the Lord the wrong way. The truth is, we're all just trying to get a job done -whether it be to build up our own house or build up God's kingdom. We all fall short and we all make mistakes along the way. A Christian may be so excited and eager to lead someone to the Lord that they may end up being condemning and judgmental, just as an inexperienced car salesman may be pushy as they're eager to put you into a new car.

A new car is great if you need one. It often depends on how we're approached as to whether or not we'll buy from an individual or even stay on the lot to talk. Same holds true for a Christian. The Lord is great and we ALL need Him. It certainly does matter that we come in a loving way to those the Lord sends us to.

Have you ever had a bad experience that has turned you off to something you were interested in?

If so, how could they have behaved to make you "buy" what they were promoting?

If we are the "pushy car salesman", let us look to the Lord as to how we could change our approach.

Dear Father in heaven, we come to You with thankful hearts. Lord, we ask you to help us with our behavior toward people. There are times we may have behaved in such a way as described in this story. There are times one bad experience may have caused us to reject everyone with the same title. Lord, remind us that we are all people. We all fall short. We are human and You love humans. That's who You sent Your Son to die for. Please, help us to remember to be kind to others. Thank You for revealing this to us. We love You and thank You for all that You are and all that You are doing in our lives. Please forgive us for our sins. In Jesus' name, amen.

Chapter Three

A Heart and a Cross

One night my daughter, who was three years old at the time, was sitting beside me drawing. I was thinking about my life. I had walked away from the Lord. I was hurt and knew I needed God. I felt I had chosen to walk away from God and He wasn't going to forgive me. I was so hurt. I thought I'd messed up and couldn't return to my Father. That fear was so far from the truth, yet I believed it! I don't know why I turned to Leah and talked to her, but I did. I told her I didn't think God would forgive me again. I had messed up so many times and I felt there was no longer any hope. She grabbed my hand and started to write on it. "No! Write on your paper, not Mama's hand," I told her. She grabbed hold of my hand again and for some reason, I didn't stop her. She began to draw on it. She drew a heart and a cross! I couldn't believe my eyes!

I was overcome with joy and amazement. I asked her what she meant by that. She didn't answer. She didn't have to. There was no doubt in my heart or mind what I was seeing was from the Lord. I knew what she meant. I knew what God meant! I looked at my hand and I felt in my heart, God had used my little girl to tell me I was forgiven and loved! What a love our Father in heaven has for us. What joy to know I fell but God lifted me back up as he did the prodigal son in Luke 15:11-32. He was waiting for me to come back to him. As He saw me coming, He ran to meet me.

What an awesome experience, even unbelievable to some, I'm sure. It was such a powerful experience. True love and forgiveness. That's what our Father in heaven is all about. God sent His Son to die on the cross because He loves us. A heart and a cross. It's open to all of us. Jesus paid our debt for us. When we truly seek forgiveness, God knows our hearts and sincerity. He comes running to meet us. He's grateful when His children come back home to Him.

Have you ever been deceived into believing God won't forgive you?

Have you ever experienced forgiveness from the Lord? Write an experience that comes to mind when you felt the burden of sin lifted off your shoulders.

Dear Father in heaven, we praise You for Your forgiveness. We thank You for having mercy on us. We sin on a daily basis, whether we realize it or not. We ask You to forgive us for our sins. Please help us to not listen to the lies we hear so loudly at times. When we feel as if we've messed up too many times to be forgiven, remind us of the truth. Thank You, Father, for Your mercy and Your grace. Lord, thank You for loving us, in spite of us. For we are nothing without You. In Jesus name, amen.

Chapter Four

Check Engine Light

One evening while cooking supper, I received a call about purchasing an extended warranty for my car. I talked to one person, which transferred me to another, then another. Usually I tell them up front I'm not interested, but for some reason I waited. The last man I was connected to said he was going to ask me some questions to see if I qualified. He asked what the mileage on the car was and if I was having any trouble out of the car. He then asked if my "check engine" light was on. I said, "As a matter of fact, it is." He asked if I knew why. "No, actually I don't. I haven't taken it anywhere to find out," I replied. He said, "Let me check to see if…" then I heard an odd noise and the phone disconnected. I guess the noise I heard was the sound of rejection. I laughed to myself as I hung up the phone and said, "I guess that's one way to keep them from calling back." In all honesty, it bothered me that he would just hang up on me without an answer of any kind.

As I thought of this call, I became so grateful God isn't like that. If our "check engine" light is on, He doesn't hang up on us. He wants to help when something's wrong. We qualify for *His* warranty by the blood of Jesus Christ. We don't even have to purchase it. The first part of 1 Corinthians 6:20 NKJV tells us *we* were bought! He paid the cost on the cross. Scripture says He bought us, therefore we most definitely qualify for the "extended warranty."

Some of us may feel, or have felt we're unable to approach the Lord for some reason. From time to time, our "check engine" light may come on. That light is so often a warning that we are separated from God or that we need His help. We should take that light seriously and go to the "Mechanic" to see what's wrong. God is the mechanic and He can fix us. When He does, we automatically want to pay Him by serving Him, hence the 2nd part of verse 20, "therefore glorify God in your body and in your spirit, which are God's."

Knowing we're bought, can you easily believe that God wants to fix whatever may be wrong in your life and heart?

Dear heavenly Father, Thank You for loving us so much that You purchased us. You sent Your Son to the cross to pay for our sin, on our behalf. We thank You and praise You for that. If there is ever a time we feel as if we can't come to You, please assure us we can. You are the Master Mechanic. Help us realize you'll continue to "fix" us until we're perfected the day we join You in heaven for eternity. Please forgive us for our sins. Fix our hearts and minds upon You. In Jesus' name, amen.

Chapter Five

Learning to Ride

My daughter learned to ride a bicycle today. Although not totally confident, she's growing with each push of the pedal. Even still, a piece of her is concentrating more on her fear of falling instead of how enjoyable riding will be. Her fear of falling became a reality as she tumbled to the ground. She bruised her leg and skinned her hands. She called it quits, but to my surprise, about 30 minutes later, she said she was ready to get back on. What time she spent riding had left an impact on her. She felt good with the wind in her hair, doing something she'd put off trying to do for so long.

You see, Leah hasn't wanted to learn how to ride a bike without training wheels for a long time. Her cousins had their training wheels removed over a year ago and learned to ride their bikes. When she saw them, she also wanted hers taken off. When she sat on the unsteady bike, she quickly decided she wanted them back on. We told her it was time to learn without them. Her bike stayed parked outside where the weather left its mark on it, leaving it rusted. She had no further interest in a bicycle until this past Christmas.

A row of bicycles was parked out front at a local store. She sat up on a pink and blue one. She said she wanted it, even though we showed her there were no training wheels on it. She assured us she was ready to learn how to ride. Christmas morning she awoke to see a new shiny bicycle parked at the tree. She quickly reverted back to having no desire to ride. Since it's been so cold, we parked the bike in the laundry room. Today was a nice day to be outside so I asked her if she wanted to learn how to ride it. She said yes!

Some of us are like Leah. We see others have so much love and zeal for the Lord. We want it too, but then as we think about it, we become scared. We allow the thought to come into our minds that we will mess up. Some let that thought prevent us from even giving it a chance, while others of us limit how far we will take the relationship. In all honesty, we will all "wreck" from time to time- some of us more often than others. The most important thing to remember is to keep our eyes on Jesus, not the fear of failing Him. Just as I ran over to my daughter and picked her up as soon as she wrecked, Jesus will pick us up, dust us off and help us back "on the bike."

In Matthew 14:22-33, Jesus walks on water and calls Peter out of the boat to join Him. Verse 30 NKJV tells us about Peter, "But when he saw that the wind was boisterous, he was afraid; and beginning to sink he cried out, saying, "Lord, save me!" Verse 31 NKJV says, "And immediately Jesus stretched out His hand and caught him, and said to him, "O you of little faith, why did you doubt?"

Whether we've been walking with Jesus just days or even years, the tide will rise from time to time. The going gets tough. Jesus always wants us to keep our eyes on Him, not on the boisterous waves of life.

Think about it. Are you like Leah?

If your fear of falling is hindering you from accepting Him or furthering your relationship with Him, remember, accepting Him is admitting we need Him- from salvation to daily life.

Dear heavenly Father, thank You for your loving us. Thank You for showing us that we aren't the only ones who have these fears. Please help us to keep our eyes on You, knowing that with You, we can do what You call us to do. Thank You for Your promises. Thank You for Your reassurance we so often need in our lives here on earth. Please forgive us when we have a hard time looking past the waves of life. Help us to focus on You. Please forgive us for our sins. In Jesus' name, amen.

Chapter Six

Lay Them in His Lap

I was in my early twenties when our collie dog, Midget, had her first litter of puppies. We had Midget for at least ten years when she first became a mother. I was married and of course Midget stayed at my parents' house where we had grown up. I went out for a visit shortly after she had her puppies. My parents had her and the pups in the house. They were concerned because she wasn't feeding them, nor did she act like she wanted anything to do with them. She wasn't behaving the way a mother would.

I was sitting in the kitchen floor with her when all of a sudden she stood up and picked her puppies up, one by one, and placed them in my lap. How odd! We all were amazed and in disbelief at what we were seeing. I remember even being a little heartbroken, thinking that maybe she didn't care anything about them. I'd never seen such! Most mother dogs feel more comfortable keeping their pups right next to them.

My parents took Midget to the vet the next day to be informed that she couldn't produce milk. She knew she couldn't take care of her pups and she knew she needed help. She looked to someone she could trust, someone she loved, and someone that she knew loved her to take care of what she couldn't.

That's the way God wants us to be with Him. 1 Peter 5:7 NKJV says "casting all your care upon Him, for He cares for you." He wants us to lay our cares in His lap. We know we can trust God. He made us!! If we were like Midget and would lay these things in God's lap, we would find that He can solve the problems that seem unsolvable. When we don't, we are starving ourselves from the peace that we could have by letting go of our cares and handing them over to the Lord. He is in control and not only can, but will resolve things righteously.

Remembering that He cares so much for you that He gave His son to die for you, list your cares you will cast upon the Lord?

How do you think you'll feel if you finally let go and let God take care of these things, trusting He'll take care of you?

Dear heavenly Father, we're coming to You in Jesus' name and we ask You to forgive us for our sins. We ask that You will help us to cast our cares upon You. We ask that You help us to leave them there and trust you'll take care of us. We know You love us and want us to be free from all these things that burden us so we can move forward in serving You. We thank You for all You do for us. Thank You for loving us. We ask that You remind us to give You the glory, honor and praise for all that You do and all that You are. In Jesus' name, amen.

Chapter Seven

Plant Parable

I looked at my plant

it was about to die.

I've neglected it-

my poor plant, oh my.

It was once so beautiful,

full with many flowers

and like my spiritual life-

I'd forgotten God's power.

As I'm convicted

in my heart of hearts,

I look close to the dirt

where I see new life start.

New leaves are growing from the old stems.

I want to shout and praise His name-

He's forgiven me once again!

We must look with our spiritual eyes

and when we don't,

our spirit surely cries.

It pants and is thirsty, it groans-but I hear

and with His love and chastening,

He once again draws me near.

It's a modern day parable

Of when we neglect Him,

our leaves dry up, we're no longer able

to produce beautiful flowers for the world to see-

His love, His hope,

His wondrous beauty in me.

Priscilla L. Bohannon

9-7-12

I received this plant when my father-in-law passed away in April 2012. At first I cared so much for it. As time went on, I stopped tending to it as much as I once had. I'd forget to water it. I'd watch the leaves as they were wilting, but I would put it off for one more day. The days turned into a week. I'd water it one day, just enough to keep it from dying, and then I'd put it off again. I repeated this cycle over a period of a few weeks. Eventually, I realized what a shame it was to see the plant look so pitiful. One day as I was out on the porch, I began to think about what was happening, not only to my plant, but to me, spiritually.

I began to water it daily and care for it as I once did. As I was taking care of the plant, I remembered when I received the plant. God had helped me get me through the pain of losing my father-in-law. I began to draw closer to Him. I saw the new leaves appearing on the plant and I began to bloom spiritually as well. One day the Lord gave me this poem within minutes.

Are you watching your plant as it slowly dies? Do you continue to put off watering it day after day?

If this is the case, God is faithful to forgive. All you have to do is ask Him. If you are dying spiritually, you can trust He can, and will, restore, revive and renew you. Lamentations 5:21 NKJV says "Turn us back to You, O LORD, and we will be restored…"

Dear heavenly Father, we want to thank You for Your love. We thank You for the sweet reminder of hope this story brings. If we've been neglecting You, please forgive us. Help us to have the courage to admit our neglect and accept Your offer to fill our basket with fresh, new leaves and beautiful flowers once again. Please help us see the need to pray for others to turn back to You as well. We ask You to forgive us for our sins. In Jesus' name, amen.

Chapter Eight

In the Fire

One evening I went into the kitchen and put a pot of tea on. I filled another pot with water to boil a couple of eggs. I was tired and had decided to fix tuna fish sandwiches for supper. I went out of the room, knowing it'd take a few minutes for the water to even begin to heat up. Before I knew it, the smoke alarm was beeping. As I ran toward the kitchen, I saw an orange glow. Fear set in. What was I going to see when I walked into the room? As I turned the corner, I saw flames shooting up toward the ceiling. I had another pot on the back burner with oil I'd used for frying and I hadn't thrown it out yet. I turned the wrong burner on and now I was in trouble.

I had heard if you throw flour on a kitchen fire, it would put it out. I reached for the flour to realize I didn't have any. I'd just used the last of it the day before. I grabbed the next best thing, I thought- cornmeal. I threw some on the pan and the flames shot higher! In a panic, I grabbed the pan and headed toward the front door. Hot oil spilled as I scurried through the house. I slipped and nearly fell, but caught myself. I took off again, holding tight to the fiery pan. The flames seemed to surround me, blowing back toward my face and body. I then screamed to my stepson who happened to be in the room, "Am I on fire? Is my hair on fire?" He looked and told me I wasn't. The look on his face seemed as if he thought I was too. I made it to the door, threw the pan in the yard and went back inside to find where grease had splashed and caught a few other things on fire. I threw the items outside and came back in.

I could've set my house on fire! I could've been badly burned! I was so relieved it was over. What was a short time seemed to have taken forever. I was most definitely thankful everything was ok but I must admit, I was shaken up by the incident.

Later, as I thought about the events of that day, I was so amazed. The flames were all around me, yet I remained untouched. It reminded me of the story of the 3 Hebrew children in Daniel chapter 3. They were walking around in the fiery furnace, yet weren't burned. Verse 25 NKJV of this chapter tells us there were "four men loose, walking in the midst of the fire; and they are not hurt, and the form of the fourth is like the Son of God." Verse 27 goes on to tell us their hair and clothing weren't affected, nor did they even smell of fire.

The Son of God was with me, just as He was with Shadrach, Meshach and Abed-Nego. I'm so thankful for the Lord's protection over my family, our home and myself while I was in the "fiery furnace".

Have you ever been in a situation where you came out "untouched?" You may never be in a fire, but a lot of trials in life are dangerous, whether spiritually, physically or emotionally. When the Son of God is with you, you will be protected.

Dear heavenly Father, we want to thank You for the stories of Your goodness. Thank You for protecting us when we have the flames of life surrounding us. Help us to share the stories we may have of Your protection, that they may bring glory to You. Thank You for protecting us daily. We love You. Please forgive us for our sins. In Jesus' name, amen.

Chapter Nine

Obedience or Sacrifice?

My daughter, Leah, was 5 years old when she had her first seizure. She and her cousin, Alana, had spent the night at my parents' house. Early the next morning we received a call from my Mom saying she thought Leah had a seizure and to meet them at the hospital. My Mom had called 911 and the ambulance was on their way. The police also came and were the first to arrive. They saw Leah while she was still seizing. The ambulance arrived shortly after and recognized her symptoms as those that are normal after a seizure-bad headache, drowsy, etc. The emergency room doctor said he thought she was having a night terror. The EMT's knew the signs of a seizure, disagreed and recommended notifying her pediatrician. I did exactly that. They didn't believe she had had a seizure so I immediately found another pediatrician. He listened to

44

me and had her scheduled for an EEG, MRI and an appointment with a neurologist rather quickly.

Less than a week later, Leah had her second seizure. She had to go to the emergency room again. This time, her dad and I took her. She didn't stop convulsing until they administered a couple of different medicines intravenously. Even after, she didn't regain consciousness. They called the local-based medical helicopter. She was airlifted to the nearest children's hospital, about 75 miles away. We received the results from the EEG while we were there that confirmed Leah had epilepsy. We were released once she was alert.

Exhausted by the time we arrived home, I plopped down in the recliner with Leah. She was sleeping as I held her in my arms. I thought the worst. I feared she had a brain tumor and was going to die. I just knew I was going to lose my baby. I started sobbing. She had so much medicine to stop the seizure that morning and was so worn out from what a grand mal seizure does to the body, my crying didn't wake her. All of a sudden a thought came into my head. I said, "Lord, You gave Your Son for us, I'll give my daughter to You if that's what You want." An instant, amazing peace came over me at that very moment! I then began laughing hysterically- just as hard as I had just been crying. It was ok. I felt peace with it. Maybe that's all He wanted to hear from me- "For You, Lord, I will."

This story reminds me of when God told Abraham to sacrifice his son, Isaac, in Genesis 22:1-13. Although I wasn't asked to take my daughter's life, I told the Lord to have His way. I thought that may have been His plan and I had peace at that very moment when I offered her up freely to Him. The latter part of Genesis 22:12 NKJV says "for now I know that you fear God, since you have not withheld your son, your only son, from Me."

Just as God spared Isaac's life, He spared Leah's life then and has many other times during her journey with epilepsy.

Thinking back, have you ever told God- "For You Lord, I will."

Did you really step out in faith and mean what you said? If so, how did it feel? If not, do you think it may be time to step out in faith and obedience, as Abraham, with some situation in your life?

Dear heavenly Father, We're coming to You in Jesus' name and we ask You to please forgive us for our sins. We want to thank You so much for sending Your only Son to die on the cruel cross on our behalf. Lord, please help us to have the faith of Abraham. To trust and remember that You love us. To remind us and help us understand that the fear You spoke of in Genesis 22:12 is obedient fear. Please help us to remember that You want obedience more than You want sacrifice. We love You. We thank You for loving us so much. We are forever grateful for Your mercy and Your grace. In Jesus' name, we pray. Amen.

Chapter Ten

I Didn't Get the Job

I received a call from the local board of education a few summers ago. The call was in regards to a job opening for an assistant in a pre-kindergarten class. I was thrilled. I told them I was interested. The interview was scheduled for a week later. I had been substituting at a local preschool and the elementary school as well. I felt confident I'd be an asset to the classroom and felt I had adequate experience. At the end of the interview, the lady said she would make her decision by the close of the day. She'd mail the notification letters no later than the next business day.

The day I expected the letter, I waited anxiously for the mail carrier. I was excited at the possibility. Not only would I enjoy the job, it would be convenient hours. To work while my daughter was at school and be off when she was would be perfect. The possibility of this job seemed to be an answer to a prayer I hadn't even prayed.

As the mail lady arrived, I stepped out onto the porch. I looked out across the field in front of my house. I watched a gentle wall of rain make its way across the field until it reached me. I had been praying the answer I wanted would be in that envelope. I pulled the mail from the mailbox, thumbed through it and found the source of my anxiousness. I knew inside there were only two possible answers- yes or no. I had hoped and prayed the answer I wanted and the answer God allowed for me would be the same. As soon as I opened the letter, I saw the word 'unfortunately'. I made my way back to the porch and sat on the swing. I looked out across the field once again. As I watched the last rain drop fall, teardrops began to fall down my face. I felt as if God had cried for me first.

Romans 8:28 NKJV tells us "all things work together for good to those who love God, to those who are the called according to His purpose." I wondered why I couldn't have been the one to get that job. As time passed, I saw reasons I didn't need to be tied to a job during that time in my life. God provided as He always does. He always will.

Can you recall a time in your life when you wanted something so badly but the reply began as "unfortunately?"

It's not always easy to accept God's will for our lives. If we are His children, we should remember He loves us and knows why we "didn't get the job." He knows why we didn't *need* the job. There are times we see why things happen as they do and other times we may not see. We need to remember God's word as it is and trust He knows what's best for us.

Dear heavenly Father, we want to thank You for loving us. There are times we may feel as if we've been let down. Please help us to remember You will work things out for our good. We are Your children. You are our loving Father. You are always watching out for our best interests. Help us to trust that You are always here to give us what we need, when we need it. Please forgive us for the times we may doubt You. Please forgive us for our sins. In Jesus' name, amen.

Chapter Eleven

Ignore

Recently I watched a video warning people of the dangers of leaving their child in a hot car. On a hot, summer day, a mother went into the store and left a small child strapped in his car seat. I'm not sure if she forgot or just thought she'd be in the store for a short period of time and it wouldn't hurt to leave him in the car. It took very little time for the interior of the vehicle to become extremely hot. As the child began to sweat, a woman walked up to the car to look at herself in the mirror. She saw the young child, but didn't rush to get help. She actually spent more time looking at herself than at the child. Another woman heard the child crying, tried to open the doors but didn't succeed. She looked around and walked off, again, without doing anything else. It was unbelievable to think people would actually walk up to a vehicle, see a helpless child, sweating and crying and not take action. A man came along and saw the child. He busted one of the windows to rescue him. Unfortunately, it was too late. The child had already stopped breathing.

Watching the video, I hurt for the child. He was crying out for help, yet people ignored him and chose to walk away. The mother either made a poor choice or a horrible mistake. Either way, she's going to endure heartache, grief and regret for the rest of her life. Sometimes our choices are life or death, for ourselves or for others.

Although I could go several different routes with this story, I feel led to write about verses 19 and 20 in the book of James, chapter 5 NKJV. It says, "Brethren, if anyone among you wanders from the truth, and someone turns him back, let him know that he who turns a sinner from the error of his way will save a soul from death and cover a multitude of sins."

With the fear of rejection, criticism or simply not wanting to "rock the boat," we often walk away from those facing eternal death. It's hardly ever easy to approach someone in this situation, but we shouldn't be as the woman that looked in the mirror at herself in the video. There's a time when our concern with the way we look shouldn't be more important than helping someone else. If we are led by the Lord to them, we must lead them back to the Lord in a loving way, focusing more on eternity than our outward appearance.

Have you ever had someone turn you back to the truth? Has the situation ever arose for you to turn someone back?

If you answered yes to either or both questions, was the situation handled in a loving way?

If not, we can always learn from ours and others' mistakes. Pray that the Lord will help us present Him as the loving Christ He truly is.

Dear heavenly Father, we're coming to You in Jesus' name. We ask that You forgive us for our sins. You know our hearts. You know if it's us or someone we may come in contact with, that needs to be turned back. Please give us the confidence, boldness and the love, to either turn back to You, or to help turn others' back. Help us remember it is You, not us, that saves souls from death. We are merely an instrument You use to carry out Your work. Thank You for all You do for us. Thank You for loving us. In Jesus' name, amen

Chapter Twelve

Name

What a joy it is when there's a little one around. How amazing to hear their little voices as they begin to talk. What a feeling of elation the moment when a little one says our name! To be so important that they would remember and know who we are. The same holds true if they've been talking and begin to grow close to you. To be recognized by a child at the most innocent time of their lives. We are real to them and it's confirmed.

I remember meeting my stepson, Eric, for the first time. He was a little over 2 years old. He hid behind his daddy's leg. He was so shy and unsure of me. It was so cute but I remember there was also a feeling of hurt because of his uncertainty of me. Even a feeling of rejection, I suppose.

Over time, he was around me more and warmed up to me. I can recall sitting in the floor at my in-laws' house playing cars with him. Suddenly, he said, "Watch Cilla!" An automatic feeling of importance and acceptance came over me. He acknowledged me enough to call me by name.

He is now 18 years old and never hesitates to call my name numerous times- even to the point I want to change it. All joking aside, when I remember this story, it takes me back and reminds me to be thankful he knows I'm here- not just when he needs me, but any time.

While we feel important when a child says our name, the Lord not only likes when we call His name, He wants us to praise His name. Psalm 148:13 NKJV says "Let them praise the name of the LORD, For His name alone is exalted; His glory is above the earth and heaven."

Have you ever heard a child call your name for the first time?

How did it make you feel?

If it made you feel good, how much more do you think the Lord enjoys us calling out His name in praise?

Dear heavenly Father, thank You for this story that reminds us that Your name is much sweeter than our own. Thank You for helping us relate to the feeling of being important to a child just the way You want to be of importance to Your children. Help us to remember how much it means to You that Your name is lifted up. Help us to know we can always call out Your name and You will help us. As we do, we are also exalting Your name and trusting in You. Father, please forgive us for our sins. In Jesus' name, amen.

Chapter Thirteen

Moving Day

My daughter had become really good friends with one her classmates, Lindsey. Maybe they connected so well because they're both shy. I talked to her teacher last week. It seems the two girls had grown close and both seemed to be coming out of their shell. It so happens, the class took a bathroom break the other day. Afterwards she realized a couple of kids didn't return to the room. The class was quick to tell her the couple were none other than the two shy ones- Leah and Lindsey. The teacher walked to the bathroom entrance to notify them the bathroom break was over. She said she almost had to turn her head and laugh because they're both so shy. They've become so comfortable with each other, they're doing things that are a bit out of character for both of them. They had developed a deep friendship. A special bond that made them forget about being shy, if just for a moment here and there. They gave each other a certain level of confidence.

Today the little girl moved several states away. When I picked Leah up from school at the end of the day, her eyes were red. I asked her what was wrong. She told me Lindsey's mother picked Lindsey up from school early today. She told me she cried in class when Lindsey left. She was truly heartbroken. She'd no longer see her friend. I held her as she cried. Knowing I couldn't take the pain away she felt in her heart, I began to cry with her. It's hard to explain to a child that things like this happen. People move in and out of our lives, and oftentimes people pass away. No matter our age, it's never easy to lose someone you love.

I can relate to how Leah feels about losing a friend. I've lost friends due to moving and unfortunately, I've lost several friends to death. I'm thankful to know there's One friend we can count on to always be here.

His name is Jesus. Hebrews 13:8 NKJV says, "Jesus Christ is the same yesterday, today and forever."

What a blessing to know, while we are going through the moves and changes in life, Jesus, our faithful Friend and Savior, never changes or moves away from us. Although we will experience sadness, heartache and pain, we'll always be able to depend on Jesus to be there with us. He wants us to become so comfortable with Him, we no longer lack, but are overflowing with confidence through Him. Not just for a moment, but a lifetime.

Have you experienced the pain of losing a friend? How did it make you feel?

How can you have comfort knowing Jesus will always be here, even if seems no one else is?

Dear heavenly Father, we come to You in Jesus' name. We ask You to forgive us for our sins. We thank You for reminding us that You've given us a friend who never leaves. We're so grateful in this ever changing life we live, we can count on You to stay the same. When we feel alone, please remind us that we're not. Give us the strength to move forward each and every day. We cannot thank You enough for the comfort You bring to us with Your promises. We love you. In Jesus' name, amen.

Chapter Fourteen

Junk in the Closet

After watching DVD's and VHS tapes for over a year, my husband decided it was time for a satellite dish. I called to order service and set up a day and time for installation. Since my house was a disaster zone, I set aside a couple of days to get things in order. They were scheduled to come the next evening. Being the procrastinator I am, I felt I had enough time without getting in too much of a hurry. I was thinking how overwhelmed I felt with all my clutter when the phone rang. It was the satellite guy. He said he was in the area and had extra time if I wanted him to come out today instead of tomorrow. I accepted the offer. I was happy for installation to be a day earlier, but I was thrown into a tizzy at the same time. The house wasn't anywhere near being finished.

He said he'd be at my house in about 45 minutes. I quickly began picking up piles here and there and putting them in the closet in my bedroom. As the minutes passed, I had to pick up my pace while picking up what was a disgrace. I began throwing and cramming everything into the closet. It was a terrible mess. Hoping he wouldn't have to go into the closet, I wiped the sweat from my brow as I opened the door for him.

I was uneasy the whole time he was here, fearing one thing would slip and there'd be a huge crash. Luckily, everything stayed in place and was safely hidden in the closet. Since it wasn't in my sight, I was able to forget about the mess I needed to deal with. Even when I did think of it, I'd shove it out as quickly in my mind as I shoved all the junk into the closet that day. I knew I'd have to deal with it sometime, yet as long as I didn't have to, I wasn't going to.

Sometimes I believe we forget that God sees all. In Jeremiah 23:24 NKJV, we read, "Can anyone hide himself in secret places, So I shall not see him?" says the LORD; "Do I not fill heaven and earth?" says the LORD." We tend to shove things out of sight and close the door on it. We know we'll have to deal with it sometime, but until we *have* to, we keep that door closed. We cringe at the thought of something falling out or crashing down, exposing our "junk," whether it be in the form of anger, bitterness, envy, pride, and the list goes on and on. No matter if we succeed in hiding it from people, God sees it and doesn't want us to keep shoving it in the closet, hiding it behind that door. He wants us to clean it up. With His help, we can!

Do you have things shoved in your "closet?"

God knows all about it. Ask Him to help you clean it up.

Dear heavenly Father, thank You for loving us. Please help us clean up the closets of our hearts and minds. Thank You for reminding us that You see all. Lord, give us the confidence to come to You for help with this.

Help us to get in the habit of picking up as we go instead of letting things pile up. Remind us that You are standing at the door with us, looking in. You're holding the trash bag, waiting for us to throw the "junk" in. We love You and thank You for all You do, have done, and will do for us. Please forgive us for our sins. In Jesus' name, amen

Chapter Fifteen

Insurance Agent

Recently I had a little insurance issue. I went straight through the insurance company instead of with my agent. I thought I'd just try to go straight to the source and do this myself. When I was told by the insurance company that I owed triple what I usually pay, I went crawling back to my agent. She said, "Why didn't you come to me first? That's what I'm here for. They are only in a hurry to get the next customer. They don't listen and they don't care." Needless to say, she was right. Why didn't I come to her first? I went to her to get the insurance in the first place, then I felt I didn't need her.

When it was straightened out, I still owed the money but she was able to get me extra time to pay it. She was kind, compassionate and helpful. I'm thankful for her and have learned to go to her first.

I thought this was relevant to Christian life. Sometimes we choose to go to someone or something else to help us. When we see we're in a worse shape for it, we realize we should've gone to God first. We still have to face consequences for the wrong choices, but God will help us whenever we decide to go to Him. God says, "Why didn't you come to Me first?" Hmmm…why didn't I think of that? Did I think I could do it without Him? Life works out much better when we go to our "Agent." God always cares. He's not in a hurry to get to the next customer. He's the Almighty! He will take care of us and He's never ready to 'let us go'.

Think about times you do things your way and times when you go to the Lord to make decisions. Which times work out more smoothly?

Dear heavenly Father, we're coming to You in Jesus' name. We ask You to forgive us for our sins. Please help us to remember to keep You at the top of our lives and come to You first. If we do happen to make a mess of things, please help us to know You are a forgiving, loving God that will help us when we come to the realization that we need You. Thank You for loving us. Thank You for helping us and bringing this to our minds. We love You, Lord. In Jesus' name, amen.

Chapter Sixteen

Change

As fall rapidly approaches
Leaves turn red, yellow, orange and brown
Then they fall, ever so gently,
To lay on the dew covered ground

It's an awakening reminder
That we'll all return to the earth
For each of us, that beginning point
Starts at our birth

It's not always easy
To accept the changes in our lives
Being a Christian, a daughter, a sister
Being a mother and a wife

But I thank You, God

For the foliage that remains ever green

I hold it dear within my view

As I sit on my front porch swing

Full of hope, it sweetly reminds me

During the seasons of sorrow and pain,

Your presence and Your love

Toward Your children never change.

Priscilla Bohannon 9/30/12

I attended a memorial service for a friend two days before I wrote this poem. It hurt me to know I'd never see her again. It's not always easy to accept changes in life. We don't always understand why things change as they do. Ecclesiastes 3:1 NKJV it says, "To everything there is a season, a time for every purpose under heaven."

When we look at our surroundings, we can hardly see anything that stays the same. The evergreen trees that caught my eye that day helped me to remember God and His love are forever. The trees may be blown down by the wind, uprooted in a storm or even chopped down someday, however, the day I wrote this poem, God used them as an example. He is everlasting in all the different seasons of our lives, just as they are "ever green" through all four seasons.

Ask the Lord to help you throughout the different seasons in life. If we look closely, we can see God is present during them all.

Dear heavenly Father, We thank You for reminding us that You love us and are here for us, no matter what season or time of life we may be in. Although it may be hard to weather the storms at times, You are there to help every step of the way. We know from Your Word, the sun will shine again. Help us when it seems life is almost more than we can bear. Thank You for the times of laughter and dance. We ask You to please forgive us for our sins. In Jesus' name, amen

Chapter Seventeen

Locked In

I'd been cleaning the house and decided to take a break when a friend called. The weather was nice so I went outside. When I came back in, my front door wouldn't shut. I noticed the doorknob was also loose. I worked with it until I finally got it to close. Hoping it would still be usable, I tried to reopen it. It wouldn't open! I was still on the phone with my friend. She was hearing my "Oh no's", so of course I told her what was going on. I said, "Great! Now I'm locked in!" Then I remembered, I have another door I could use in the laundry room. The door was blocked with bags of bottles and cardboard I hadn't taken off to the recycling center. It wasn't going to be as easy or convenient as the other door, but there is another way to get out of the house.

1 Corinthians 10:13 NKJV is about temptation. The latter part of the verse says "but with the temptation will also make the way of escape, that you may be able to bear it." I thought of this verse shortly after the doorknob was broken. I found it relevant to the situation I had found myself in. I'd have to walk an unfamiliar path. I'd have no choice but to move the things that needed to be moved long ago. The door I'd have to go through is one so rarely used, I'd forgotten it even existed, however, I was reminded of its availability when I came to my senses.

Although we're not all tempted by the same things, all of us *do* face temptation. What hope it brings to know God supplies us with a way out! We can choose to remain "locked in" and unable to move on, or we can use the other door He's provided. We may have to move some things out of the way to get to the other door, but with Him, it *is* possible.

Think about the temptations you may be facing. Pray for God to give you the faith and courage to escape.

Don't forget to praise Him for the help He gives you. As you praise Him, He will give you strength for each step in the right direction.

Dear heavenly Father, thank You for providing us with a way out and making it bearable. It may take us off the beaten trail a bit, but there *is* a way to "get out." Please help us to seek You as we face temptation. Help us to remember Your words and to write them on the pages of our hearts. Lord, help us to draw strength from You to take the "other door." We love You. We thank You for showing us hopeful truth. Lord, forgive us for the temptations we give in to and help us to move forward with You. Please forgive us for our sins. In Jesus' name, amen.

Chapter Eighteen

Fireworks

One Sunday afternoon my husband, Jason, my stepson, Eric, and myself were sitting outside. Eric had several packs of stink bombs and firecrackers. Suddenly he threw a stink bomb at the Jason's feet. It then became an all-out war. They proceeded to pull out the firecrackers and I was quickly drafted. I was unarmed, which wasn't fair at all. I jumped off the front porch and ran around the house with my cup of tea, trying to escape the line of fire. My husband caught me as I was coming around the other side. As he was lighting the firecracker, I knew I'd have to defend myself. All I could think to do was throw my tea on him. He paused and looked at me in disbelief. If anyone was shocked at the events, it was me! My husband was throwing firecrackers at me for goodness sake!

I took off, hoping to make my way indoors where I'd be safe. With Jason running swiftly behind me, I ran up a hill in the backyard. Mid way up, I fell. It was one of those falls like you have in a dream. You know the one. Someone's chasing you, you fall but can't move to get up and get away. I looked down. I was on my hands and knees, on the ground, empty cup in my hand, still upright, I might add. Once I was finally able to stand, I turned to see Jason doubled over, and Eric, who's now also armed and dangerous. They were laughing so hard that I didn't have to worry about being hit- at least not until they regained their composure. The war ended shortly afterwards. Thankfully I was able to escape, unharmed, as I made my way indoors.

As we live the Christian life, we're spiritually attacked. Ephesians 6:11-17 tells us to put on the "whole armor of God" and tells us how and why. Verse 11 NKJV says "Put on the whole armor of God, that you may be able to stand against the wiles of the devil." It's important to be prepared for an attack at any time. Verse 16 NKJV speaks of "the fiery darts of the wicked one." By no means do I consider Jason and Eric the "evil one", however, this passage comes to mind when I think of the situation I suddenly found myself in. When we serve the Lord, we are open targets for spiritual attacks. If we put on the armor of God daily, we will be able to stand.

Have you ever been attacked spiritually? Were you prepared?

If not, you can use this as a learning experience to know the importance of being prepared. Remember, an attack can come at any time, therefore we must be ready at all times.

Dear heavenly Father, we come to You in Jesus' name. We ask You to forgive us for our sins. We thank You for telling us how to stand strong and be prepared for the "fiery darts" that come at us as we live the Christian life. As we study these verses, help us to memorize them . Help us to remember to dress ourselves in this armor, just as we dress ourselves each morning. Thank You, Father, for loving us. In Jesus' name, amen.

Chapter Nineteen

How Many Times

As a mother, it seems I'm always getting on to my daughter. I can recall many times as I'd be making the bed, she'd put her head under the sheet. I'd always say, "How many times do I have to tell you to stop doing that?" The other night, what once was a stack of books by the bed became a strewn mess all over the floor. I said, "How can you do that and not let it bother you?"

So many times it's as if I hear God say to me as soon as the words leave my mouth, "That's what I'm asking you!" How many times does God have to tell me not to do something and I do it anyway? How many times do I do something and not let it bother me? So often, the questions we ask our children may be the same questions God is asking us. We, at times, are to God as our children are to us. Maybe we aren't listening, or we don't allow ourselves to be bothered by His questions. Our children oftentimes don't want to face it and give us an answer. Sometimes we don't want to face it and answer God's questions to us. Some of you may not have children. I'm sure you had parents, grandparents or some authority figure in your life, as a child, you had to answer to.

God is the ultimate authority regardless of our age. He loves us as we love our children, or as we are loved by those that cared for us when *we* were children. He, at times, asks us questions because He loves us. He wants us to think about what we're doing and decide if it's the right thing to do. Hebrews 12:6 NKJV says, "For whom the Lord loves He chastens, and scourges every son whom He receives." He corrects us, or gets on to us, because He loves us!

Can you remember a time you had to be told repeatedly to do or to not do something? If you have children, do you catch yourself asking your child or children that- "How many times…" question?

Listen as the Lord may be talking to you. He wants to prepare you for the work He calls you to do for Him on earth. He wants you to be ready to live with Him in heaven when He calls you home. Let us be thankful, even as adults, we have Someone watching over us.

Dear heavenly Father, thank You for caring for us so much that You will discipline us. You want us to be obedient children. Please help us to be open to Your questions and willing to change our ways as our answer. Thank You for loving us. In doing so, like a parent, You correct us from time to time. We thank You for reminding us why You correct us. We are thankful You love us enough to call us out when we need correction. Help us to look to You as an example of how to raise our own children. Please forgive us for our sins. In Jesus' name, amen.

Chapter Twenty

Him, Not Me

You're not mocking me,
You're mocking Him-
The One who died
For all our sins.

The nails in His hands,
The nails in His feet-
The blameless One
They whipped and beat.

You're rejecting Him,
Not me-
The One who's blood
Sets us free.

You're hurting us both

Because I love Him so.

When I suffer with Him

I'll receive a crown of gold.

Not that I want it,

You'll see if you read-

I want those crowns

To lay at Jesus' feet.

Priscilla L. Bohannon

9-23-12

It's not always easy to hear the comments made to you when you love the Lord. In Matthew 5:10 NKJV, Jesus says, "Blessed are those who are persecuted for righteousness' sake, for theirs is the kingdom of heaven." When we are mocked and made fun of, we are joining Christ. Of course we know He was persecuted. We must also remember these words of Jesus in Luke 23:34 NKJV- "Father, forgive them, for they do not know what they do."

All hearts aren't ready to accept Jesus at the time we wish. Personally, I have to keep in mind I was once was in those shoes and had rejected Him or anyone that served Him. I'm thankful for how merciful God is. When I made my decision to ask Jesus into my heart and life, He didn't reject me as I had once rejected Him. That shows the character of God. He's patient and kind. His grace is bestowed upon us before we ever ask Jesus into our hearts. Isn't that amazing?

Have you ever been mocked for standing up for the Lord?

Have you ever mocked someone else that stood up for Him?

Although we may take it personal, it's only because we love Him so much. We need to remember, it's not about us, it's about Him.

Dear heavenly Father, we're coming to You in Jesus' name. We thank You for being patient with us before we made the decision to follow You. Remind us of the possibility that the ones that make hurtful remarks may be fighting a battle against and within themselves. You may already be working on their hearts and *they* may not even know it. Help us to remember it's about building Your kingdom, not ours. Remind us to pray for these people. We thank You for bringing this to our minds. Help us to show the love You have for all the world- saved and unsaved, giving encouragement for the saved and hope that the unsaved will join you in eternity one day as well. Please forgive us for our sins. In Jesus' name, amen.

Chapter Twenty-One

Devotional Prayer for Care

What if you were the one in the wrong

And you were the one left standing alone?

If no one would want to talk to you

And you had no one to help you through?

Who would God use if no one will forgive?

Who would be around to show Jesus lives?

If He's forgiven you, can you forgive another

Whether it's a stranger, son, daughter, or brother?

Would you long for someone to do what's right?

Would you wish for someone to shine Jesus' light?

Lord, please give us the words to say,

Help us work for You today.

Could you love your neighbor as yourself?

Could you lead that lost soul away from hell?

Lord, put love in our hearts to spread the Word.

Lord, help us shout it so Your voice will be heard.

Help us walk with You, the One that is above.

Help us to show Your precious compassion and love.

Help us to hold each of our thoughts captive.

Help us tell the enemy he can't have this.

Help us remember we all need prayers.

Help us to show others that You care.

Remind us that love covers a multitude of sins.

Lord, help us to see that true love always wins.

Help us imagine standing at those heavenly gates.

Help us to help others before it's too late.

Help us to give others another chance.

Thank You for going through the same song and dance-

With us all

As we fall

Day after day

Yet You continue to show us the way.

Lord, you are so patient and kind.

Lord, please help us to keep this in mind.

Lord, please forgive us for all of our sins.

In Jesus' holy name, amen.

Priscilla Bohannon

4/26/09

Revised 6/30/14

Ephesians 4:31-32 NKJV Let all bitterness, wrath, anger, clamor, and evil speaking be put away from you, with all malice. And be kind to one another, tenderhearted, forgiving one another, even as God in Christ forgave you.

Colossians 3:12-13 NKJV Therefore, as the elect of God, holy and beloved, put on tender mercies, kindness, humility, meekness, longsuffering; bearing with one another, if anyone has a complaint against another; even as Christ forgave you, so you also *must* do.

1 John 2:10-11 NKJV He who loves his brother abides in the light, and there is no cause for stumbling in him. But he who hates his brother is in darkness and walks in darkness, and does not know where he is going, because the darkness has blinded his eyes.

Mark 12:31 NKJV "And the second, like it, is this: 'You shall love your neighbor as yourself.' There is no other commandment greater than these." (-Jesus)

Matthew 10:27 NKJV "Whatever I tell you in the dark, speak in the light; and what you hear in the ear, preach on the housetops." (-Jesus)

2 Corinthians 10:5 NKJV casting down arguments and every high thing that exalts itself against the knowledge of God, bringing every thought into captivity to the obedience of Christ,

1 Peter 4:8 NKJV And above all things have fervent love for one another, for "love will cover a multitude of sins."

Chapter Twenty-Two

Mountains and Valleys

While I'm standing atop the mountain
Do I peer down into the valley below,
Or do I look past it to the next peak
As the hope I have as I onward go?

If only my constant strong point would be
To gaze upon the higher terrain
Maybe going through the valleys
Wouldn't be such a horrible strain.

Atop the mountains, the Son seems so close
The natural warmth and peace I feel.
While heading downward into the dark valley,
With aching bones, I begin to feel winter's cold chill.

As I'm climbing up out of the valley

I shed my blanket, feeling the warmth again.

If only I were content with the climate changes

Because I know, walking with me is my Friend.

So on my spiritual hike of life

And with spiritual eyes open, I see-

He is my blanket when I am cold

And when I'm warm, He's carrying it for me.

Priscilla L. Bohannon

7/8/14

One early May evening, my husband borrowed his brother's motorcycle. He and I went for a peaceful ride in the country. As we cruised down the road, I looked out at all the beautiful things God had made. The trees, the grass, the clouds - everything so wonderfully perfect. We stopped and got off the motorcycle to walk around a little bit, then decided to head toward home.

The temperature had dropped as the sun was setting. It was comfortable sitting still, but as we traveled downward into the valleys, we could feel the cool air. I wished I would've worn a jacket. I was so thankful as I'd look ahead of us and see a hill. I knew I'd feel the warmth once again, if only for a moment. How much warmer it felt after being on the lower ground. We continued on our ride, knowing it was the only way we'd make it home. We'd have to endure the cold drafts along the way.

I began to think of life. Christian life to be specific. Things aren't always warm and cuddly. We suffer sometimes. We must remember although we may feel helpless, we aren't hopeless. We're on our way toward another mountain. Just as the experience on the motorcycle, I knew I'd have to endure the cold valleys. I knew I'd have times of warmth that didn't last as long as I wanted them to. I had to endure the climate changes, the good and the bad, to make it home. That's the way Christian life is. We have to endure the times in the valleys. We know we have to travel the path of hills and dips in order to reach our home. Our final destination, where we cannot begin to fathom the level of eternal comfort. Heaven- where we'll be with our Creator that offers the hope as we travel on our way, even in the coldest times.

Are you on top of a mountain or are you in a valley?

Study the word of God and pray to Him. Make the prayers to Him personal, as if you're talking to a friend. After all, He *is* your friend.

Dear heavenly Father, We love You. We admit, we don't understand why things do or don't happen. We don't understand why we have times when we feel so far down in the cold valley. Lord, please remind us that You are with us. Help us to feel Your presence and Your peace. Help us to feel the warmth of the blanket of love and hope You have wrapped around us. Lord, please give us the strength to make it to the next mountain. Push us upward to the peak once again. Help us to praise You no matter where we are on our hike in life. Lord, please forgive us for our sins. In Jesus' name, amen.

Chapter Twenty-Three

The Lampshade

As I was sitting on the couch in the wee hours of the morning, I heard the sound of bugs buzzing. Earlier we had gone to the store. As we were carrying the groceries in, the door was left open. A couple of bugs had flown inside, drawn in by the light from the floor lamp behind the couch. They were flying around the light bulb in what is a funnel-like lampshade. The shade is frosted plastic, so as I looked up behind me, I saw the bugs that I'd been hearing. They were making a strong effort to get out. I watched their shadows as they climbed midway up the shade, only to reach a certain point and slide back down.

What was once so attractive to them had become the exact thing they were trying so frantically to escape from. They had found it to be dangerous and harmful to them. The heat from the bulb was too hot. Maybe they knew if they were left there, they would be added to the pile of dead bugs that have collected at the bottom of the shade.

I decided to turn the lamp off as I was saddened by their situation. Almost as soon as I did, the buzzing stopped. A few minutes later, I looked up to see one bug still at the base of the shade running around. He didn't take advantage of the opportunity to escape. He didn't feel the heat anymore and was content staying where he was. The other bug was circling the rim of the shade. He chose to escape when he had the chance. He was only on the lampshade for a short time. As I continued watching him, he flew away and left the area completely. I didn't see where he went, but he came to his senses and left what had hurt him. To my knowledge, he didn't return. Maybe as he was circling the top of the shade, he was looking at what he'd escaped from, then made his decision to flee from it. I went to bed and didn't turn the lamp back on until the next day. I found myself wondering if the bug at the bottom finally flew away also, or if he chose to die there with the others.

I thought of myself and others' allured by sin. So many things look appealing to us as human beings, yet they're dangerous. Not only physically and mentally, but most importantly, they're dangerous to us spiritually. When we take part in sin, we begin to feel the heat from it in some form or another. We so often want out, and may even try to climb up, yet we continually slide back down into the very base of the lampshade time after time. We even continue to slam ourselves into the scorching bulb, over and over again. We buzz and make noise just like the bugs. We're calling out for help.

Every day we have a choice to serve God. We may find our current place of residence in a lampshade. As the day comes to a close, the Lord turns off the lamp for us. He gives us another day to make a decision. He gives us yet another day to make the choice to stay in the place we're in, circle the area, or fly away to a safer place - which is with Him.

Maybe those bugs were blinded, dizzy and exhausted from the heat the lamp was giving off. Maybe they were even confused and not able to figure out how to get out of the situation they were in. The only true and everlasting source of help comes from the Lord. Psalm 121:1-2 NKJV says, "I will lift up my eyes to the hills- from whence comes my help? My help comes from the LORD, who made heaven and earth."

Are you in the lampshade and can't get out?

Although we may have gotten into a situation we shouldn't be in, the Lord is there to help. He's there to lead us away from the scorching bulb we can't seem to get ourselves away from.

Dear Father in heaven, thank You for loving us. Thank You for reminding us that our help comes from You. You made the heaven and the earth and all that is in it. You don't want us to continue doing what hurts us. Lord, we thank You for helping us see what You want us to see. Thank You for Your hopeful word. Lord, turn off the power of the source drawing us in. Give us the strength to climb up out of the lampshade, the courage to look down at what You've brought us out of, and the power to fly away from it and never return. Please forgive us for our sins. In Jesus' name, amen.

Chapter Twenty-Four

Approachable

When I go into a store, restaurant or even just a group of people, I often feel as if I'm not welcome there. People snub their noses at me or act as if I'm a bother them. As I walk into a local grocery store, I sigh with relief when I see a certain lady working the register. She doesn't treat me as so many others' do. She doesn't look at me as if I'm a nuisance or unworthy of her service. She smiles, makes small conversation and laughs. She treats me as if I'm a person. She treats me in a way that makes me feel good about myself.

Sometimes, I believe, we become so consumed with the way people treat us, we base our value on it. We let it scar us. If we are children of God, we know our value- His Son. Sometimes, we may say we love, we may quote scripture, but I wonder, do we really understand? Do we even know how we make people feel? As we go about our Christian lives, do we forget the very core of the birth, death and resurrection of Christ? It was because of love! Yes, even those of us that represent Christ, (Christians - which means "Christ like") fall short of this terrible case of inapproachability and hatefulness.

If we make this attitude a habit, how are we ambassadors for Christ? Do we find it hard to show love for the unsaved? Do we even have love for our brothers and sisters in Christ? 1 John 4:20 NKJV tells us "If someone says, "I love God," and hates his brother, he is a liar; for he who does not love his brother whom he has seen, how can he love God whom he has not seen?"

Why do we so often see people try, and sometimes succeed, at belittling others- making them feel unworthy of the very breath they're taking, when each breath we are *all* given is a gift from God? 1 Corinthians 13:1-3 tells us about serving God without love. It doesn't amount to anything and is nothing more than a loud noise such as a clanging cymbal. Verses 4-8 tells us about love and its characteristics.

We're all guilty of handling things the wrong way. Unfortunately, I'm guilty too many times. I do believe, however, there is a fine line when it comes to our handling situations. Sometimes we have to be stern to make sure it's understood where we stand. At the same time, we are told to do it in love. Of course we come in contact with those that will take advantage of us being a Christian, saying we aren't allowed to do anything but stick our tails between our legs. The way we handle situations are often rejected by others, even if we have prayerfully approached the situation. If we follow the Lord's guidance, although everyone may not be accepting, it's of utmost importance to please Him.

We've all been hurt, wronged and treated unfairly, but we can turn it around and see that we are all guilty of these offenses as well. We may find it helpful to remember, it is our job and our passion to show the world Jesus. If the world is full of unapproachable, unloving people, how will we show others Christ and His love? The first 6 words in John 3:16 NKJV says, "For God so loved the world..." There's love. If that's why God sent His Son, Jesus, how do we go on making people feel uncomfortable, unworthy, unloved, condemned, and hated?

Do you believe the Lord is approachable?

What our human emotions feel and our human eyes see isn't always the correct representation of the Lord, the way He feels about us, the way He treats us, or the way He wants us to be treated.

We treat others badly at times. Think of how you may treat people and the damage that is done to their hearts due to your actions and/or words. Ask the Lord to forgive you. Ask Him to help you approach someone you've mistreated and sincerely apologize. I've found this to not always be easy, but many times the person will forgive you and you'll feel much better righting a wrong.

Dear heavenly Father, we're coming to You in Jesus' name and we ask You to forgive us for our sins. Lord, we are sorry when we treat others' in a negative way. We ask You to heal our hearts from the hurtful way we are often treated. Please help us remember to look to You as our strength and our shield. Please remove and guard us from bitterness, hate, spite, and any other disease that tries to seep into our hearts. Help us to be kind to others'. We know we will slip up from time to time. Please Lord, help us remember Your love for us, no matter if we do. Help us to be able to love, forgive and see other people as You do . Help us to gain more of Your character daily. We love You. We thank You for Your deep love for us and reminding us, You ARE love. In Jesus' name, amen.

Chapter Twenty-Five

Reflections

It was mid July and had been an extremely humid summer. It had stormed the day before, which had cooled things off and seemed to have completely erased the humidity. I'd have to say it was almost cool as I sat on my front porch that morning. As I was looking around at the greenery, a certain brightness above me caught my eye. It was a shimmering light on the ceiling of the porch. I wondered what was making the beautiful sight I was seeing. I looked down beside me at my dark cup of coffee. I knew it had to have been something clear and pure. I looked down to the left of me at the dog's water bowl. No sunlight was shining on it, so I continued searching. I looked over to my right and saw that the gentle wind was blowing the water that had collected in the bird bath from yesterday's rain. The light of the day was shining upon the water. It's shimmering reflection was what I had been seeing.

I began thinking of the reflection of the water. I'd already been reflecting upon myself while sitting in the calm of the morning. My actions, my appearance to myself and to the world- those close to me and those who see me passing by here and there. I'd been reflecting on my heart. A scripture then came into my mind. Proverbs 27:19 NKJV- "As in water face reflects face, So a man's heart reveals the man."

As the breeze of the morning ceased, the reflection sat still. I noticed it wasn't as beautiful and majestic as it once was when the wind was blowing. It had created a cool, smoke-like appearance. It made me think of the calm times in life. It's easy to be happy and content in times when all in *my* little world is going well. When the wind blows and things are no longer calm and still, the wind oftentimes blows our hair in our faces and blows debris in our eyes to keep us from seeing. It's then that our reflection should be even more majestic and beautiful.

The beauty seen in those moments isn't of us. It's the wondrous beauty of the indwelling power of Christ in our hearts shining through. If He is in our hearts and our hearts reveal the man (or woman), our reflection should have an alluring beauty. So alluring that it causes others to look and to be amazed. It should make them become so curious that they have the urge to search for what's causing the beautiful reflection they're seeing. When the wind is blowing, or in other words- when our faith is tested- the joy and glory of the Lord should be revealed. We should have the reflection of an illuminating light that is breathtakingly beyond words.

Think of looking into a still body of water and seeing your reflection. Imagine the wind beginning to blow. As you keep your eyes fixed upon the reflection of your face, you see the water begin to move. You no longer have a clear visual of your face. You are no longer able to focus on your outward appearance. We then have the opportunity to focus on what's inside. What we're really made of. The inner most secret part- our heart.

Do you see the peaceful ripples in the water? Do you see beauty in your heart as you are no longer able to see your face?

Dear most gracious heavenly Father, You are so kind to give us such a peaceful example. Lord, help us to see a beautiful reflection. Help us to be shimmering and majestic on the inside. Help us to be mindful that the beauty seen is the reflection of You. Lord, if we're discouraged when the wind blows and distorts our faces, help us to remember it's not the reflection of our face You want us to focus on. You want us to look within ourselves- within our hearts. Our heart reveals who we truly are and it is *there* that You look . Help us to see the breezy times as times of reflection. If we aren't truly happy with what we know You see, please make it beautiful. We thank You for Your love. We thank You for all you've ever done for us and what You continue to do. Please forgive us for our sins. In Jesus' name, amen.

Chapter Twenty-Six

Blackberries

Early into our marriage, Jason and I had a Rottweiler. We had received word that someone needed to find him a home because they were moving. He was about a year old when we got him. He was big but gentle. His name was Mack. He came into our family while we were in the process of purchasing our first home- a mobile home. We had cleared out an area on top of a large hill in the woods for our home to be placed.

While bulldozers were busy and wells were being dug, we would walk around the land quite often with Mack following alongside us. One day while walking, we found a few blackberry bushes along a path past the edge of our yard. We began picking berries and eating them. Mack decided to pick some as well. We laughed as we watched the large dog pull berries off the bush and chew them up. We didn't expect a dog to eat blackberries, much less pick them himself. As we picked and continued watching him, he picked a red berry. He quickly spit it out of his mouth. We also found that quite humorous. We pointed to a few blackberries and he picked them and happily ate them. A few minutes later, another red berry was being spit out onto the ground.

Although it's been about 15 years ago, I still think of Mack around blackberry season. I had the pleasure of visiting a blackberry farm a few weeks ago. I'd already been thinking of Mack and his reaction to the unripe berries. This made it much more real and heavenly as I looked at all the rows of ripened berries. I'd been thinking of what the bible says in Revelation 3:16 NKJV about a particular church. "I know your works, that you are neither cold nor hot. I could wish you were cold or hot. So then, because you are lukewarm, and neither cold nor hot, I will vomit you out of My mouth."

I don't want to be vomited out of the Lord's mouth for being a "lukewarm Christian." I want to be what *He* wants me to be- hot and on fire for Him! Just as we were pointing to the ripe berries for Mack to enjoy, the Lord can point us towards ripening for Him to enjoy, therefore, not vomiting us out of His mouth.

Do you feel as if you may be a sour berry- or lukewarm?

Dear Father in heaven, we're coming to You in Jesus' name. We ask You to please forgive us for our sins. Lord, we thank You for Your love and Your warnings to us. Help us to understand You do it out of love to continue in the perfecting process of our lives in order to ready us for Your kingdom. Lord, if we are lukewarm, please, help us to change our temperature. Help us to become so hot that we're on fire for Your truth, Your love, Your perfecting process. You and everything that has to do with You. Help us to not take bits and pieces from Your word, but to honor *all* You say. It can only be done with Your help and our openness to Your guidance. We love You, Lord. Please show us the way. In Jesus' name, amen

Chapter Twenty-Seven

Blessings Do Abound

Some are blessed with talent
Or many years of good health,
Some with a large family,
Some, an abundance of wealth.

Some short, some tall,
Some with curly hair,
Some with deep compassion
That always show they care.

Some may be blessed
With humor or quick wit
Some have the blessing
Of being able to forget.

Some have been blessed

With many true friends

Some see they have blessings

That seem to never end.

Some show lots of love

Some show much patience, indeed

Some show the world Jesus,

Some are led to believe.

Some may have a bountiful feast

Some may share a song

Some that see themselves as weak,

Others see as strong.

Some may have equal parts

Of sunshine and of rain

Some may learn to live is Christ

And to die is gain.

No matter what we have

It's given to us in love

All the things that are given to us

Are given from our Father above.

So Lord, please remind us
If we forget they can be found
There's something good, if we only look
Because blessings do abound.

Priscilla Bohannon
6/2014

1 Corinthians 12:12 NKJV says "For the body is one and has many members, but all the members of that one body, being many, are one body, so also is Christ."

We all have different gifts. We are all made differently. The body of Christ must work together to accomplish what the Lord has set out for us to do. It's not just the body in one church building. It's not just one race. It's not just women or just men. If we are Christians, we have family all over the world. We must unite to do what we should for the Lord, no matter if we're near or far away. No matter if we have differences, past or present, we're all aiming to reach the same destination and our Father is the same. Until the time of arrival at our destination, we are to be united, passing out invitations for others to join us in building His kingdom.

Dear heavenly Father, we're coming to You in Jesus' name. We ask You Lord, please forgive us for our sins. We thank You for reminding us that You've made each of us the way You wanted. You've given us each certain gifts to point others toward You. Help us to be thankful for what You've given us and who You've made us to be. Help us to see the need to work together for Your kingdom's growth. Lord, if we don't know where our place is or we can't see what gift we're holding, please reveal it to us so we can use it to fulfill *Your* work through us. We love You, Lord. We thank You for loving us. Thank You for using us. Help us to always be willing. In Jesus' name, amen.

In loving memory of Beverly DeBerry-Hill 8/1/57-6/24/14

Chapter Twenty-Eight

Egg Hunt

This past Easter, my sister had an egg hunt at her house. On the count of three, the kids darted off in hopes to fill their baskets full of candy-filled and coin-filled plastic eggs. We watched all three children run past the eggs that were placed at the starting line. They were so excited and focused on the hunt, they chose to hunt instead of gather. They didn't notice what was practically handed to them. I heard just about every adult there comment on how the kids ran past the simplest finds. After the eggs were becoming scarce to find, the kids then had to canvas the area to find what they hadn't noticed before. With help from the adults pointing them out, they were able to gather the remaining eggs.

We are sometimes like kids at an egg hunt. The simplest things are right in front of us, yet we run past them, almost as if to say, we'd rather do things our way. We see the kids passing the simple finds as they're hurrying along, focusing on the task of filling the baskets. We, too, sometimes fail to stop and look to see what's right in front of us waiting to be picked up. God is giving these things to us, yet we run past them. It's almost as if we want the hunt instead of gathering what He's laid before us to fill our own baskets.

As the adults pointed out the eggs the kids had failed to see, we must look to the Lord to point out the things He is giving to us. We can't look to *people* to find God's will for us and our lives. Colossians 1:9-10 NKJV says, "For this reason we also, since the day we heard it, do not cease to pray for you, and to ask that you may be filled with the knowledge of His will in all wisdom and spiritual understanding; that you may walk worthy of the Lord, fully pleasing Him, being fruitful in every good work and increasing in the knowledge of God."

Are you as a child on an egg hunt?

If so, pause to look at what you may have ran past. Pray for the Lord to give you discernment with each choice you make. Everything that's in front of us isn't necessarily God's will for us.

Dear heavenly Father, we're coming to You in Jesus' name. We ask you to forgive us for our sins. Lord, please help us to look in front of us to see what you have laid out. Help us trust *You* instead of venturing to find what *we* want to find and how *we* want to find it. Please help us to remember to look in front of us and pick up the treasures you've laid within our reach. Help us to have discernment to be able to know when the things we see are from You. Lord, You're so gracious and loving. Thank You for all You have done, are doing and are going to do. In Jesus' name, amen.

Chapter Twenty-Nine

A Heart's Silent Prayer

As I lie here

And I begin to pray,

I bow my head

With no words to say

From thoughts to speech,

I haven't a clue

My heart seems to know

But the words won't flow through

I have to know nothing

As intercession's made for me

I can only cry out

From my heart, a silent plea

Guilty, I am

And others at times

But the only heart

I can surrender is mine.

Forgiveness You offer

While others' may not

I need You to cleanse in me

That which has set up to rot.

The cross I carry

As I stumble and fall,

Falls upon me

Lift it Lord, hear me call.

Consequences, I know

I will face, with no doubt

But please, lighten the load

Lord, hear my soul shout!

Lately I've been

Where I do not wish

The cup not passing from me,

But no comparison to Your dish.

Pick me up, Lord,

Help me along

I admit I am weak,

I proclaim You are strong!

Priscilla Bohannon

7/13/14

Sometimes, when we are broken and exhausted, we can't find the words to say when we go to the Lord in prayer. It happens to me quite often. You know what? It's ok! Romans 8:26-27 NKJV tells us, "Likewise the Spirit also helps in our weaknesses. For we do not know what we should pray for as we ought, but the Spirit Himself makes intercession for us with groanings which cannot be uttered. Now He who searches the hearts knows what the mind of the Spirit is, because He makes intercession for the saints according to *the will of* God."

Have you ever been stumped with what to say during your prayer time with the Lord?

How do you feel knowing it's ok if you ever are at a loss for words?

Dear heavenly Father, we thank You for loving us. We are so thankful to know that we have help with our prayers. We don't always know what to pray. We're thankful that You're all-knowing. Thank You for being such a great help to us, during every time in our lives. Thank You for showing us how mighty You are. Father, if Your children are ever unsure whether or not You hear our prayers, even if they are silent, please remind us of this scripture. We thank You for every single thing. Please forgive us for our sins. In Jesus' name, amen.

Chapter Thirty

Big Trucks

Growing up, I lived on a dirt road in the country. For many years of my life it was a single lane road. They eventually widened it to make it two lanes. After I moved out and was married, they tarred and chipped most of it, including in front of my parents' house. The better the road conditions, the more traffic. It's still a rural area, but more people travel the road now than ever before.

Last week, my Dad and I were sitting outside. We watched as dump trucks sped down the road and dangerously around a curve in front of their house. They were carelessly driving in the middle of the road. Later in the week, I took my daughter out there to stay while I went to the dentist. My Mom text me before I left and told me to watch for the dump trucks. They were going up and down the road again. During that week I turned my lights on bright, even though it was daytime. I made sure to be over on my side of the road as far as I could get. I was driving with extreme caution. I knew there was a chance I'd meet a dump truck and I wanted to be prepared. I wanted to be safe!

Today I went out to my parents' house again. I remembered the dump trucks but Mom didn't mention anything about them traveling the road this week. I still watched and was careful but I didn't have my lights on. I guess you could say I was more lax today than I had been the week before. Last week I knew for sure there was a possibility I'd be meeting a large truck speeding down the middle of the road. Today I wasn't so sure.

As I came up on the curve in front of their house, I came face to face with a large, white truck. It wasn't a dump truck but it was large and it was taking up too much of the road. I had to get off the road into the grass quickly. I was thankful I was aware enough to take action. I was thankful for the Lord keeping us safe. I'm reminded of what I already know and need to do- to ALWAYS be watching!

As I think of watching, I think of scripture. Jesus speaks about His return in the book of Mark, chapter 13 verses 32 and 33 NKJV. He says, "But of that day and hour no one knows, not even the angels in heaven, nor the Son, but only the Father. "Take heed, watch and pray; for you do not know when the time is."

In life, we never know what's coming around the curve toward us. We have to be prepared! The same holds true with the coming of Jesus. I was given a warning by seeing the trucks and my Mom warning me about the chance of meeting them. We are given a warning by Jesus Himself regarding His return.

In the same chapter, verse 37 NKJV, He says, "And what I say to you, I say to all: Watch!"

Are we watching for Him?

Dear heavenly Father, we thank You for all Your blessings. We thank You so much for Your word. Lord, help us to understand that you warn us because You love us and we're so grateful for it. Help us to be ready for Your return at any time. Help us to take heed to Your warnings. Help us to remember to Watch! We thank You for keeping us safe during life and giving us yet another day to draw closer to You. Please forgive us for our sins. In Jesus' name, amen.

About the Author

I was born the last of 5 children. I grew up in Middle Tennessee and still reside here. I am married to Jason Bohannon. I have a stepson, Eric, and a daughter, Leah.

The stories in this book are very personal to me. You see, the Lord has given them to *me* first. These are lessons He's teaching *me.* There has also been a lot of healing with the stories and poems in this book. He's the Almighty, yet He speaks to me simply through everyday life. He's blessed me with the ability to express what He's given me through writing and He's made it possible for me to be able to share it with you.

My Dad has used his artistic talent to draw the pictures for this book, which makes it even more special. To have my earthly father working with me to glorify our heavenly Father is such a blessing.

I pray that you will find the stories in this book inspirational and that each chapter will touch your heart and draw you closer to the Lord and His love for you. He *will* help you to see that in every situation, He's there!

Galatians 6:14 KJV But God forbid that I should glory, save in the cross of our Lord Jesus Christ, by whom the world is crucified unto me, and I unto the world.

All glory to Him!

Made in the USA
Charleston, SC
03 October 2014